IN
LUST

The Key To
Visual Communication
& Brand Marketing

....

ANGI EGAN

INITIAL LUST

Initial Lust – The key to visual communication and brand marketing.
© Angi Egan.

ISBN: 978-1-906316-22-8.

All rights reserved.

Published by Word4Word, Evesham, UK. www.w4wdp.com

The right of Angi Egan to be identified as the author of
this work has been asserted by her in accordance with the
Copyright, Designs and Patents Act 1988.

A CIP record of this book is available from the British Library.

No part of this publication may be reproduced in any form or
by any means without permission from the author.

Printed in the UK by TJ International, Padstow.

Very important —
this copy belongs to
lovely Liz Holmes —
ger off..!!

Keep shining!
Angi

Preface

Preface

I first became involved in high street retailing as a sixteen year old Saturday girl. I learnt from the best over my 20+ years in retail and now understand some of the basic principles of successful retailers and businesses – buy for the customer, remain focused and disciplined, keep control, offer the right stock and, above all else, avoid corporate thinking!

Comprehensive change on the high street and in business today demands what many would consider radical behaviour – a true passion for your product and a fanatical understanding of who is going to want to buy it.

Too many businesses have had an inflated view of their ability to provide outstanding service and great value products. This is their downfall. What must now happen is a return to great service from interested, enthusiastic and knowledgeable individuals who understand the product they're selling and, more crucially, recognise which product will best meet their customers needs.

And business needs to be decisive. Confidence and belief inspire trust and loyalty from customers but the key is to remain consistent. Consistent in what you offer, what you stand for and how you're going to deliver it. Failure to do this leads to dilution of confidence and customers will soon start to look elsewhere for what they want.

The principles outlined in the first of the *Romancing the Customer* series shifts the focus from corporate thinking and places it firmly back to where it should always have been… on the customer.

Angi Egan

······
Dedication

Dedication

To Martin Dobbs – the best mentor, friend and business confidante I could have ever been lucky enough to work with. You watch my back, encourage me and kick my ass at just the right moment – thank you.

To Paul Whitehouse – a creative genius, inspiration and excellent drinking partner. Unsure if I'll ever forgive you for introducing the Guinness and port – awhh the hangover! Still think Langley Brothers are figment of your brilliant imagination by the way…

To Lizzie Cheney – blessed to have you in my life. The bestest mate I could ever wish for – thank for all that you are x

Finally, to the businesses I have been privileged to learn from, who have been open to the craziness I bring and who have been the inspiration behind Romancing the Customer – thank you from the very heart of my bottom!

Contents

	Introduction	13
CHAPTER ONE:	Visual Communication & Brand Marketing – an overview	21
CHAPTER TWO:	Visual Communication	27
CHAPTER THREE:	Big and Bold	33
CHAPTER FOUR:	Creating Visual Impact	43
CHAPTER FIVE:	Office Environments	57
CHAPTER SIX:	Websites	65
CHAPTER SEVEN:	Liberate the Retail Area! Open Versus Closed Merchandising	75
CHAPTER EIGHT:	Conclusion	87
	About the Author	91
	What People Say About Angi Egan	95

Introduction

Introduction

Initial Lust is the first in a series of books exploring the principles adopted by iconic, consistently successful businesses. These businesses appear undaunted by an increasingly saturated market. They are neither anxious nor discouraged by the challenge of institutionalised imitation. They understand exactly what it takes to turn their customers into raving fans.

They will be obsessive about upholding the principles that have stood the test of time, because they understand one thing – they work!

Everything within the Romancing the Customer series focuses on the need for businesses in the 21st century to create lasting relationships with their customers.

Mind share

So many businesses have concentrated on market share and have missed the one thing that will offer them not only that elusive differential but also consistent profits through word-of-mouth and viral marketing – that of mind share.

The measure of success for many businesses has been the number of new customers they have attracted, while missing a critical aspect… the number they have been losing! Having new customers as your principle measure of success means existing customers become cynical and feel taken for granted. This is the equivalent of being treated like a one-night stand – they get what they want and then become disinterested in you. This is a disaster for relationships and a costly mistake for businesses.

For your customers, great service is a given. Great products are also a given – after all, we now have so much choice. Customers must now be provided with inspired expertise. They must leave a little smarter than when they arrived.

And this requires passion and a dedicated knowledge of your product or service. Beyond this, developing a fanatical understanding of the customers' individual needs, wants and desires rather than yours (or those of your business) is something that will have customers falling in love with you and your brand.

Rewarding relationships

Your challenge is to keep them in love with you. Adopt the principles of Romancing the Customer and you will enjoy not only long lasting, rewarding relationships with your customers, but you'll also have amazing fun in the process.

Too many businesses have an exaggerated notion of their ability to provide outstanding service. Harsh but true. So many times energy, finance and time are poured into initiatives that customers simply don't care about or are, indeed, not interested in.

This results in perceived indifference and costs industry on average 35% of their revenue – a major chunk of money by anyone's measure.

INITIAL LUST

It is the equivalent of guys focusing time and energy on paint jobs for the car but failing to be impressed by replacement throws and cushions in the home. We assume so much about the priorities and somehow forget to ask and check things out. We're tuned into radio WIIFM (what's in it for me).

Romancing the Customer is focused on achieving two goals:

- Creating more customers, who spend more money and who rave about you to their contacts

- Reducing the attrition of customers through addressing their needs – and in the process reducing the attrition of valuable team members because they are adding value, having fun and being empowered to do amazingly nice things!

This may be a soft skills issue but its message is deadly hard – increase the service level, surprise and delight your customers, focus on the differential and you will automatically drive profits.

INTRODUCTION

Romancing the Customer looks at each of the five senses and identifies where the parallels exist in business. Initial lust, or visual marketing, is the first step in creating this sensory experience.

The purpose of this first book is to provoke an increased client-focused business and a renaissance in service.

Romancing the customer is about:

- Keeping customers in love with you and your brand

- Providing them with inspired expertise

- Understanding that while soft skills are required to achieve this, the message is deadly hard.

CHAPTER ONE

......

Visual Communication & Brand Marketing – an overview

Visual Communication & Brand Marketing – an overview

Romancing, when done well, is a total sensory experience. It taps into our emotions rather than our intellect, and is responsible for seducing and persuading the object of our desire to fall in love with us.

Business, like romancing, when done well, is a total sensory experience. Service excellence and successful brand delivery is where the notion of romance applies to business – irrespective of the service or product being supplied.

> *"You know it's love when every touch is electric"*
> Anon

Great brands are obsessive about their customers (in a healthy way rather than a scary bunny boiler kind of way). Their every thought, every action and total commitment is focused upon how to capture the imagination and ultimately the customer's spend.

Appealing to both sides of the brain

Everything we communicate visually is processed through the left side of the brain, which is responsible for logic and reason – critical when it comes to supporting the emotional, instinctive responses processed through the right side of the brain.

Left brain function uses logic, is totally detail oriented and is where facts reign supreme. The main stimulus is from words and language, order and pattern. The left brain is entirely reality based and enables us to form strategies that are both safe and practical.

Right brain functions, on the other hand, use feeling and are almost entirely "big picture" oriented. This is where imagination rules, especially when symbols and images are used to represent a message. Right brain is almost totally fantasy based; presenting us with possibilities that appear to render us susceptible to risk taking and impetuous behaviour.

VISUAL COMMUNICATION & BRAND MARKETING – AN OVERVIEW

Appealing to both consistently is perfect for lasting relationships and, coincidently, for successful sales.

Reflecting brand quality

Visual communication includes not only our environment; it also includes how we present ourselves as a brand. All printed literature from brochures to despatch notes, your website and your business cards need to consistently reflect the brand quality.

This can NEVER be compromised, even in the name of BTN (better than nothing). Rather like remaining in a relationship because it's better than nothing, compromising on the quality of your brand simply to get something out there is no justification.

This is the first step towards unwittingly damaging your brand. It always undermines your authority and results in a loss of customer confidence. It's never worth it and, I'm sure you'll agree, certainly not BTN.

For a perfect, lasting relationship it is important to understand that:

- Service excellence and successful brand delivery is where the notion of romance applies to business

- Great brands are obsessive about capturing the imagination and ultimately the customer's spend

- Brand quality should never be compromised.

CHAPTER TWO

······

Visual Communication

Visual Communication

Compromising, or worse still ignoring, the visual aspect of every element of your business is, I believe, a sign of commercial insanity. But then I would say that, I'm in the business of visual communication.

Seriously though, visual communication is often the first thing a potential client experiences with any brand. What does yours say about you? Are you communicating in a way that directly weakens your authority by using poor quality visuals and printed materials? Is the literature you produce inundated with grammatical errors and spelling mistakes? Or is everything you do a positive and accurate reflection of the quality you aim for?

Visual clichés

You have on average two to five seconds of a customer's attention before they move on to the next thing vying for their interest. Therefore your visual messages must be compelling through using humour, headlines, colour or powerful imagery. If you use a visual cliché you are guaranteed to be creating zero impact… it's just so predictable.

For example, the ubiquitous hot stones on a naked back for spas, or the glossy smile and a headset for call centres – in fact every profession has its equivalent visual cliché. Ensure you're not using your professional cliché.

Dare to be different because the alternative is just plain dull and boring.

> *"Never let what you cannot do interfere with what you can do"* John Wooden

There is, however, a balance to be met. One of my principle roles when I joined The Body Shop was to act as a commercial voice to the brilliant designers based in London. They created award-winning designs, which were worthy of a place in any of the capital's galleries, and their passion for their art was tangible. The problem came when the designs were

VISUAL COMMUNICATION

then moved out of the studio and into the high street stores – they were just too complicated!

Being too clever

While the designs were stunning, commercially they didn't work because the concepts or messages were far too clever. They lost the opportunity to make an immediate impact. As soon as the designs developed into simple and direct visual images they just worked. Not particularly inspiring for the designers but it sure kept the stores happy.

Also hold in mind becoming too 'in-house' – this is where copy develops into the equivalent of an in-joke that no-one understands except for the brand. And it's not about you – it's all about the customer. Using trusted external sources to test your ideas will pay dividends in the long run.

The alternative is a marketing or promotional campaign that satisfies the ego of the marketing department while doing little for the sales. Avoid this indulgence – it costs brands thousands.

It's about
the customer!

- You have on average two to five seconds to hold a customer's attention so your message must be compelling

- Dare to be different but don't be too clever

- It's not about the marketing department – it's about the customer.

CHAPTER THREE

......

Big and Bold

Big and Bold

As I've already mentioned, you have an average of two to five seconds to stand out from the crowd with your visual messages. Now I'm a fervent reader and have been from a tender age, however, in that time I can only manage about five words. So the message needs to be short and sweet, and big and bold.

As soon as there is a flood of text you have lost the customer's attention. Especially in an environment where there are competing messages.

Use visuals to help customers navigate the space – remember "a picture paints a thousand words" is never more appropriate than when communicating a message. It cuts through the fog with laser-like precision and creates far greater impact. When accompanied by compelling copy, it builds anticipation and is totally irresistible.

Finally, the message must be consistent. Imagine a red thread is running through everything you do – how many times does it get broken?

The red thread begins with the windows or business frontage. This is often the first time your message will be seen. It must be stunning. It has to create mystery. And it must stand out.

Given that you tick all of these boxes you will have captured the imagination of the customer so they feel compelled to enter your store/showroom/salon… but you have changed the message inside! The red thread has been broken and as a customer I either forget why I came in so leave, or become deeply frustrated because I'm interested but feeling lost.

Seamless seduction

Either is undesirable – it's comparable to clumsy fumbling and that's deeply unattractive! The seduction needs to be seamless, confident and totally sublime.

BIG AND BOLD

Ensure you continue to communicate the same message, in the same way, with your internal signage. It's the visual equivalent of a treasure hunt – to keep a customer intrigued it must be consistent and it must be simple to follow. Repetition of your brand and the promotional message is critical to its success.

All too often businesses decide to mix their messages. This is borne out of a belief that failing to do so means customers will miss something. I figure they are going to miss it anyway – simply because you're saying too much. There is no clarity to what you're saying – it's like a visual mumble.

"Good enough never is"
Debbi Fields

It is better to pick a lead product or service and major on this. You can always then decide to layer the lead message with a smaller promotional message. Just ensure you have a strong red thread to begin with. Avoid falling into the trap of introducing too many layers – it will create visual pollution and this undermines your authority and destroys confidence.

There is another benefit of selecting one message at a time to major on and that's the opportunity to change it on a regular basis. This maintains customer interest, which stops them becoming bored. If you always have the same old message, it eventually becomes wallpaper so is subsequently ignored by the customer.

Think about how successful retailers have a promotional or marketing campaign in their stores. With a little thought and creativity you can replicate this when communicating the services and products you have on offer.

Make it relevant or seasonal in the same way retailers do. Accountants could major on personal tax returns on the approach to January 31st to avoid hefty fines for late returns, dentists could create a sense of urgency before holiday times and Christmas to get a check-up and avoid expensive call out fees. Whatever your profession or industry, there

BIG AND BOLD

will be trends. Identify these and use them to create new customers as well as new messages.

This also establishes you as the source of expert knowledge – they may not have considered the consequences until you made them aware with your campaign. Be the one who provides inspired expertise, it has a powerful effect.

Non-verbal communication

It is also important to hold in mind that customers' measures of our competency are rarely, if ever, determined by how brilliant we might be at something. It is almost always measured and judged by what we're saying through non-verbal communication.

How clean the business facia or entrance is will set the tone for everything that follows. What does it feel like to receive your brochure or printed literature? How minty does the hanging signage look, or the magazines, the coffee machine, the toilets, the fitting rooms, the mirrors – absolutely every aspect of what a client experiences visually will be sending out a powerful message about your competency and the degree to which you care, whether this was your intention or not.

Avoid falling into the misguided belief that no-one will notice the dog-eared sign, the peeling wallpaper, the broken Perspex holder, the grubby, stained coffee machine or your frayed collar and un-ironed shirt – they will and they do, and you will pay the price by communicating the wrong message. It rarely suggests how fabulous you are.

The mind of the customer

Having a passion for detail and an obsessive, fanatical eye for standards will enable you to view things through the eyes of the customer. The perception of our quality and ability to provide fabulous services and amazing products resides in one place – in the mind of the customer.

So the visual communication in your office, factory, showroom or store needs to be reviewed critically on a regular basis. And don't forget you and your team.

BIG AND BOLD

Great businesses, especially in retail, understand that the more relaxed we are the more time we spend in their environment. This means more opportunities to tempt us into buying more than we planned, or to communicate our additional products and services. The key to this depends on how comfortable and enjoyable the experience is.

And also how easy it is for them to understand the message you're communicating. "Dwell time" is directly correlated with sales, so if you create a more pleasant environment and increase dwell time, sales rise.

Effective visual communication means customers feel confident and therefore good about buying into your brand. It communicates how great your products are and it means customers never have to work hard in the process. Make no assumptions about the amount of time people have to browse – your communication needs to be clear, easy to understand with just a hint of more to come.

Seduce your customers with your brand by:

- Keeping your messages short and sweet
- Keeping them consistent
- Changing them on a regular basis to make them tantalising
- Developing a relaxed and enjoyable environment that encourages "dwell time".

CHAPTER FOUR

······

Creating Visual Impact

Creating Visual Impact

We are bombarded with thousands of messages every day so care is needed to ensure that your message is eye-catching and highly seductive. This begins with ensuring that there is a consistency in everything a customer sees.

Everything you expose customers to visually must help them understand which is the right product or service for them. The alternative is a customer who feels confused. And confused customers say no every time.

Visual pollution

Creating this highly valuable consistency begins with identifying what your lead service or product is and major on this. So many times I see businesses confusing their offer by promoting several things at the same time. As a customer I simply can't choose,

I'm unable to focus and so I zone out and focus on what I'm there to buy and nothing else.

In business I see companies and consultants listing endless services on their business cards (more on these later) and literature in the mistaken belief that as a customer I'll be impressed by their varied services.

The opposite, in fact, is true. I have no idea what it is they're good at. They appear unconfident about themselves and their expertise and so unwittingly communicate in a way which leaves me confused and doubting their credibility. I'm simply left feeling overwhelmed by the different messages.

"Having a simple, clearly defined message can capture the imagination and inspire passion. It can cut through the fog like a beacon in the night"
Sam Parker

CREATING VISUAL IMPACT

It does little to create anticipation and irresistible temptation either. It's the equivalent of baring all and leaving nothing to the imagination. You surprise and delight your customers far more by introducing additional products and services in an appropriate and relevant manner, rather than attempting to explain everything at the same time.

Better to find the judicious opportunity to unfurl your breadth of services and products in a thoughtful manner than to pitch everything at once in a desperate and frantic manner. Clarity in communication is the key to successful sales.

The message being communicated must be consistent and clear – this ensures you maintain credibility, authority and customer confidence. Consistency is persuasive and commercially successful and helps to produce great visual communication that says "you know you want to" rather than "look but don't touch".

INITIAL LUST

It is a genuine way of communicating how great your brand, your products and your company are.

This is not confined to the window or the reception area. It includes every piece of printed material you create – posters, adverts, fliers, business cards, pricelists, appointment cards, dispatch notes, email etc.

Have a process in place which allows quality checks to be made on every communication that leaves your business. This will guarantee that your brand values and integrity never become compromised or undermined. Let's pick two of these:

Business cards

- Decide what it is you want to communicate with your business cards – do you want to tell all or just hint at what you offer? This is often the first thing people see in a business environment or networking event. It is the first opportunity you will have to create the wow factor

CREATING VISUAL IMPACT

- Consider also the ergonomics of your card – it must be able to fit into a wallet or business card holder. Designing something that is non-standard is flawed – if it can't be filed it will be dumped! Confine non-standard shapes to your promotional material not your business cards

- Ensure you use both sides of your business card. It is a missed opportunity and a false saving to only print on one side. Don't be misguided – use every available space

- Ensure they are professionally printed. This is a necessary investment – substandard cards suggest you either don't take yourself seriously or worse that you won't be around very long. This may not be your intention but it certainly is what gets communicated.

Advertisements

> *"Describe the sizzle not the sausage"*
> Anon

- All too often the headline opportunity is lost because this is where the business or individual's name gets placed. This is OK if your name happens to be highly marketable (Madonna, Beckham) or your brand name is highly prestigious. However, for the majority it will be the service we deliver or the offer we have that needs to take centre stage

- Headlines need to occupy 25% of the overall ad space (or more) and be at least three to six times larger than the main body of text. This will make it a very powerful visual element that flags the reader's attention

CREATING VISUAL IMPACT

- If the company logo is used then it should be positioned appropriately – at the bottom of the advert not the top!

Create a template to guarantee you create eye-catching headlines to capture the hearts and minds of your target market. Ask yourself:

- Does the headline or opening paragraph offer key benefits? It needs to have a benefit-related intrigue or news value rather than simply making a statement – the sizzle aspect not the product, eg FEEL GORGEOUS, SAVE TONS, SLEEP BETTER, BE FREE FROM PAIN, MAKE AN IMPACT, INVEST FOR PROFIT? Whatever it is that your service or product provides must form the lead. And if you don't know – think about it

- What is the key benefit of using your product or service (save money, save time and effort, have pleasure, relieve tension, create glowing skin, protect your investment, feel divine etc)?

- Is the headline personal, ie does it have the words 'you' or 'your'? This is not always necessary but it can be effective

- Does the headline use appropriate flagging words that instantly get the attention of your target audience – mothers, teenagers, stressed, fatigued? Remember you have an average of two seconds so it must be a maximum of two to three words

- The headline may need a word specifically related to the product or service, eg holiday, back pain, lose weight, bright teeth, natural tan, perfect nails, tax return, aching joints etc

- Is the overall theme effective and does it have the right feel for the specific campaign, eg is it fun or indulgent, does it carry authority etc?

Visual impact guidelines

The graphic materials need to flag the reader down the page – this is where photographs, coloured text etc need to be placed

Do not be tempted to use more than two different type faces or too many colours as this just looks cluttered and unprofessional

Use any photographs, logos and illustrations to break up the copy. This acts as visual punctuation and helps people navigate their way to the main messages

When you have finished creating an ad walk away from it, do something else for 10 minutes, then come back to it and assess what the first thing is that captures your eye. Was this your intention?

If not, time to tweak. If yes, fabulous!

Is there a direct call to action?

Finally, the ad or promotional message must tell the reader what to do next to take advantage of this great offer. This sounds obvious but it's always the obvious stuff that gets forgotten.

Always remember – difference attracts. This might simply be your enthusiasm, which is always refreshingly different in today's business world.

More on the red thread...

The way to create a constant, clear and informative sales message is to identify any "show case" opportunities that may exist in your environment, and then use these to maximum effect.

Such "show case" areas are vital for creating a consistent message for the visiting client – a virtual red thread – which strengthens your brand authority by communicating who you are and what you do, in a style that is consistent and comprehensive.

CREATING VISUAL IMPACT

This can be achieved by the careful and deliberate positioning of products and images to convert a customer's want into a need. This is fundamental to all of the decisions we make when deciding to part with our hard-earned cash.

Customers and clients need to know not only what it is they are looking at, but what it's for, why it's great for them and where they can buy it. Countless times we are exposed to images and displays that look good but don't tell the complete story. This is a missed opportunity.

One last point on the benefits of consistent communication is the amount of time and effort a customer has to 'invest' before they are able to buy something – whether this is a retail product, a hotel room, a professional who can explain the services, or a meal in a restaurant.

It is worth holding in mind that when customers are made to wait their impression of your overall service plunges; irrespective of how great the experience has been up to this point or how brilliant your products are.

Create the
wow factor
with your visual
communications by:

- Identifying what your lead service or product is and majoring on this

- Completing quality checks on every communication that leaves your business

- Incorporating your brand guidelines into the induction programme

- Not forgetting the red thread – it strengthens your brand authority by communicating who you are and what you do, in a style that is consistent and comprehensive.

CHAPTER FIVE

......

Office Environments

Office Environments

These can easily become like a home from home for your team. One of the most challenging aspects of creating an environment that feels 'team friendly' and professional is striking a balance between the two.

I worked in an office years ago that had a very strict policy for office protocol whenever there were visitors. Surfaces and desks were cleared to within an inch of their life, candles were lit, fresh flowers were bought, clothes were ironed to a starched finish, lipstick was at the ready – in short, we were all put in fear of our lives if there was so much as a paper clip out of place! Think *The Devil Wears Prada* and you wouldn't be far off the mark!

Authenticity

Yet this wasn't authentic and it certainly wasn't real. And guess what? The visitors were aware of it and my guess is they left feeling uncomfortable, unconvinced and concerned about the genuine personality of the brand.

The extreme is an office environment where the desk becomes a shrine to the individual occupying the space. There is the hybrid collection of pigs on the desk, the computer screen is obscured by intimate family snaps, and there are the ubiquitous 'fun' notices that announce that being 'mad' somehow qualifies you to work there. In addition, there is an ocean of tatty handwritten notices announcing the latest office policy on replacing the toilet roll when it runs out and there is a lingering fragrance of food heated in the staff microwave for lunch.

Think cosy, comfortable, careworn – the equivalent of baggy trackie bottoms and you will be near the mark.

Seeing your environment through the eyes of your visitor is one of the hardest things to achieve. It's inevitable you're going to become familiar and 'blind' to what others see, but it's not impossible.

OFFICE ENVIRONMENTS

> *"Being challenged in life is inevitable, being defeated is optional"* Roger Crawford

Creating a floor walk document that details minimum standards and areas to be checked on a daily, weekly, monthly basis will ensure you're experiencing things as your visitors do.
Have a clear policy on what is acceptable to have on the desk, what can be warmed through for lunch, and what signage is acceptable (branded, framed, typed, professionally printed would be the minimum).

You also need to have a policy on what magazines should be kept in the reception area, who is responsible for replacing them, and what the artwork or visuals are around the office. All of these standards will protect your brand identity and ensure you're communicating the right standards for your profession.

INITIAL LUST

Make a checklist

Introducing a checklist will give you a fresh pair of eyes. I compare it to the feeling I get when I return home following a period working away or being on holiday. That moment when I first walk through the door… for the first minute or so my home feels a little unfamiliar; it's almost as though I'm experiencing it for the first time. This is what visitors are seeing, smelling, touching, hearing – is this what I intended?

Or when an unexpected guest drops in at a moment's notice, do you fly around tidying up to create the right image, or are you perfectly content that the look and feel is the one you were aiming for?

It must be authentic, totally reflective of you and real – this is what I mean by balance. This is no different to our office environment.

OFFICE ENVIRONMENTS

If you were to take a virtual tour around a truly professional business environment and then you were to return to look at your office through the same eyes, how would it look? Be brave enough to make the changes necessary to project an image of your business that is truly reflective of your brand quality – even if it does mean sending the little piggies home!

Your office environment should:

- Not become a home from home for your team
- Be professional – but also authentic
- Reflect your brand.

CHAPTER SIX

......

Websites

Websites

There is one simple way to summarise where the focus should be for your website – **it's not about you!**

Almost without exception (and we'll look at the exceptions) websites are focused on the business and not the visitor or potential customer. They are no more than an online brochure and generally a pretty dull one at that.

The dullness begins with 'welcome to our website'. If the objective of a website is to stand out, be visually stunning and appeal to your target customer – to create differential – then you just fell at the first hurdle.

Everyone starts with 'welcome to', except the top ten websites in the world who understand that they must build relationships by focusing on the needs of their audience and not bore everyone silly with a history of the company. You know the sort of stuff – when you were founded, where

INITIAL LUST

you're based, what you do, the hierarchy, where you qualified or what letters you have after your name. People simply don't care. Harsh but true.

Even worse are the sites who, in an attempt to appear 'right on', present the whole team in an overly matey style. It's rather like the guy who wears humorous ties or cartoon socks to demonstrate how funny he is. It's not!!!

Websites must provide information about the service or product – that's why people are searching in the first place. They're looking for the expert, the specialist, or the brand that offers the knowledge and the information they're after. And they want it fast. I learnt recently that most individuals never spend more than 0.5 seconds flicking through a website to establish if it's "the one". This is a terrifying statistic, yet illuminating too.

In exactly the same way as you need to create visual impact and pattern interrupt with your printed material, your virtual visual marketing needs to be just as dynamic.

WEBSITES

To connect on the web you need to speak the language of the people you're aiming at by using their tone, words and colours. This is the beginning of the relationship. You need to understand what people expect, so ask them and stop assuming you know.

Become obsessive about what words people use to find your services (and they're rarely what you imagine them to be), be relevant with your language and content, and be up-to-date, otherwise your very shiny, expensive website becomes relegated to the BTN category and is damaging your brand and costing you money.

> *"Be a good listener. Your ears will never get you into trouble!"*
> Frank Tyger

Now it's critical at this stage to point out that what I know about websites and techie stuff is limited to an instinctive feel about what works rather than any real knowledge about SEO/SEM/ISP or any other three letter acronym associated with IT. For me it is akin to the dark arts – I know it exists but I don't want to learn it.

I shall, for my benefit if for nothing else, keep things really simple. It appears there are three main areas to concentrate on with your website design and it is nothing more complicated than colour, words and pictures.

Colour

I know there will be men reading this who may think "that's typical of a woman" but it is nevertheless true. If people expect your profession, product or service to be a particular colour then it makes sense to be that colour, or at least a tone around this (I also know guys don't do shades so perhaps speak to a woman!). For example, if I said garden materials what colour immediately comes to mind? Green and brown would be my guess. If I said accountants you might think dark blue. In either case you wouldn't be thinking pink.

WEBSITES

This is what I mean by know the colour your target expects you to be – ask, don't assume.

Words

These are not your words, they are the words people use to find the 'stuff' you do. What are people searching for? Having these key words on your website and on the header page will ensure you're one of the first sites pinged up by Google or Yahoo (pinged up being a highly technical term that I just invented). There are all sorts of wonderful free gizmos to help you track words, try wordtracker.com as your starter for ten.

If nothing else, your website needs to use the terms, references and language of your target audience otherwise you'll cause them to disconnect in an instant. Be relevant and up-to-date with the language you use to communicate and employ a copywriter to translate your jargon and blurb into something resembling interesting content – it will be worth it.

Pictures

We all know the maxim "a picture paints a thousand words" – well it's true! Have pictures of your product, subject, service or profession, although avoid the visual clichés already mentioned in the visual communication section. If you have about half a second of a customer's attention before they decide you're not "the one", then visuals must play a central part of your home page.

Think about making the visuals humorous, create headlines and use colour. Also, think about a visual metaphor for what you do – just create powerful imagery. Remember visual clichés are guaranteed to create zero impact, whether they are the ubiquitous hot stones on a naked back for spas, or the glossy smile and headset for call centres. Every profession has its equivalent visual cliché – ensure you're not using yours.

This is as technical as I get on websites. I simply wanted to introduce this as a vital part of your initial lust thinking. It is in many respects more important

WEBSITES

than any printed brochure (sorry printers who may be reading this), simply because it is so often the first thing clients use to find you. Its impression will either create a connection or drive the object of your desire into the arms of another. In today's world the visual aspect of your website and its accompanying content is becoming increasingly critical to your credibility, success and authority as the 'go to' business.

Be clear about one thing – if it's all about you and it fails to deliver nuggets of information and inspired expertise then you might just as well donate your cash to the Angi Egan benevolent fund for all the good you'll be doing your business.

Oh, the exceptions in case you're wondering, are Google, Amazon, Yahoo, YouTube, Facebook, Wikipedia, MySpace, BMW, banks, supermarkets etc… None of these have even a hint of cliché or "here's all about us" because everything is focused on the visitor. Learn from the top 6% – it only works.

Remember your website is not about you!
It is about:

- Customers looking for the expert, the specialist, or the brand that offers the knowledge and the information they're after

- Creating dynamic virtual visual marketing

- Creating a connection immediately. If you don't you will drive the object of your desire into the arms of another.

CHAPTER SEVEN

......

Liberate the Retail Area! Open Versus Closed Merchandising

Liberate the Retail Area – Open Versus Closed Merchandising

It's hard to overemphasise the importance of open merchandising in the retail environment. I still see retailers who lock everything behind glass cabinets and showcases. Keeping merchandise behind locked cabinets guarantees that purchases are being prohibited.

You can have the best product range in the world, with the most seductive merchandising displays, but if the customer can't pick things up, it's a complete waste. If customers are unable to experience the product, they just won't buy.

Customers buy things today more than ever on touch and play. Apple stores do this brilliantly without compromising security. It is vital for a customer to experience the product for themselves. They want to know how it feels and how easy it is to understand. More critically, it allows the customer to imagine what it is like to own one (remember the power of the right brain to create images and seduce us into impetuous decisions).

Emotionally connected

Although you can demonstrate the product to your heart's delight, customers need to see for themselves how fabulous they are by touching and experiencing for themselves. As the retailer you demonstrated and talked about it, now it's their turn! In retailing the 'possession' or sensory experience of a product is the critical issue. Once a client has the product in their hand they become emotionally connected, paying for it then becomes a trivial point.

Selling is the main reason for stocking retail products in the store. Obvious huh? So make them as accessible as you can. Countless times I see products locked away in darkened cupboards. It's almost as though the decision to retail a particular brand turns the stockist into the role of secret agent. We won't share the fabulous products on offer but assume the customer will ask if they want something – they won't!

Making retail products as available as possible also creates an opportunity to up-sell and create link sales. We need to be able to compare one product against another; otherwise we're limited to taking only what we're aware of. There is no opportunity to tempt ourselves with additional or complementary products. We need to take advantage of the unique opportunity we have to educate our customers about our products, along with the need to communicate how this benefits them. This means many will spend more than they had intended.

Another aspect of liberating the retail area is to create logical adjacencies – the placing of one item next to another to create interest and increase the average spend. This is the major part of what adjacencies can deliver – add-on sales.

Sometimes this is just the usual till point 'impulse buy', but add-on sales can take place anywhere that products are available. Specially created impulse purchases or promotional offers typically have a high profit margin, and they can make the difference between a business that just gets by and one that prospers.

Making merchandise inaccessible damages your business in other ways too. There is a fine balance between making something beautiful but precious and untouchable – you allow the customer to like what they see but stop them from getting involved with the product. This is precisely what you don't want in a retail area where the objective is to encourage people to pick things up and take things home.

Accessibility

Customers have become accustomed to retailing environments where everything is accessible and on open display, with great promotional material

LIBERATE THE RETAIL AREA – OPEN VERSUS CLOSED MERCHANDISING

giving them all the information they need. I don't know about you, but I always assume something is expensive if the retailer hasn't priced a product, and I certainly won't ask. Firstly it requires effort and secondly the fear is that it is out of my price bracket and I don't want to look a fool.

Much of the reluctance by retailers to throw open the locked door of the retail cabinets is the fear of people pinching the products. This is, sadly, a fact of retail life and so needs to be built into the depreciation line of your P&L. It is, however, not all misery. To begin with, the up-turn in retail sales more than compensates for the loss from theft. If it didn't we wouldn't have successful retailers on the high street.

> *"Life is not about waiting for the storms to pass... it's about learning how to dance in the rain."*
> Vivian Green

There are also any number of security cameras that can be installed cost effectively that act as effective deterrents. However, my belief and experience has shown that the most effective deterrent to shrinkage or theft from the retail area is to ensure all staff acknowledges the presence of every customer.

This has a wonderful way of welcoming a genuine customer and a very effective way of letting a potential thief know you've seen them. This can be a simple hello or can be a direct comment about the product they are looking at.

As a slight deviation at this point I make a solemn appeal that no-one ever greets a customer with the four most useless words in retail: "Can I help you?" It is just so lacking in imagination, is totally naff and does nothing to create a fabulous retail experience.

Anyway, it is almost always met with a "no" from the customer and shows no enthusiasm for the product or your brand.

LIBERATE THE RETAIL AREA – OPEN VERSUS CLOSED MERCHANDISING

Customer profiles and stunning windows

This may sound like an obvious comment but you need to know who your customer is in order to retail successfully. This not only involves decisions about the products you stock but also about where you position them.

High street stores and retailers in shopping malls need to use every available opportunity to capture the imagination of passing trade. This begins with your windows and needs to follow through to the signage in-store.

The investment in hiring the professional services of a visual merchandising specialist will pay for itself ten-fold in the battle to stay ahead of your competitors. Window displays and internal cabinets need to communicate your retail and promotional message and using a visual merchandiser will ensure you create window campaigns that have high impact and are memorable.

Countless times I see poor window displays that will be costing that business thousands of pounds because they look jaded and boring – don't let your business be one of them.

The promotional or product message needs to be big and bold and short and simple, otherwise it's lost. Marketing messages in the window need to be read in an instant, no more than two or three words. Studies have shown that, on average, signs get less than two seconds exposure per client. That's not many words!

Humour and charm

Use humour and charm to delight the customer, making your windows not only a commercial success but a critical necessity in defining the customer experience of your brand.

Use your promotions to build a little visual anticipation. With the promotional signage,

LIBERATE THE RETAIL AREA – OPEN VERSUS CLOSED MERCHANDISING

first you need to get a customer's attention. Once you've done that you have to present your message in a clear, logical fashion – a beginning, middle and an end.

People will then have an opportunity to absorb the information a little at a time and in the right sequence. You have to capture their attention first otherwise nothing that follows will register. Too much information too soon and they become overloaded and give up. Finally, as I've said already, if you confuse the customer they will ignore the message altogether.

Repetition is critical to the success of promotional messages – several different messages result in confusion. This means you lose credibility, authority, customer confidence and increased sales and profitability.

You **won't** increase your sales by:

- Keeping merchandise behind locked cabinets
- Using the four most useless words in retail: "Can I help you?"
- Having poor window displays.

CHAPTER EIGHT

......

Conclusion

Conclusion

Businesses must avoid assuming anything as this leads to the equivalent of clumsy fumbling – the insensitive gesture, or the thoughtless word that means the object of your romance disconnects, or worse, it destroys the moment and they leave you.

Businesses that can anticipate their customers needs, that never take them for granted and that remain obsessed with creating wow moments will be the those that have shifted their focus from market to mind share… in other words: ask, ask and ask some more.

The reasons for romancing the customer are no different to the world of relationships. Once we've captured the heart, we've captured the person, they've fallen in love with us and we want to keep them. We certainly don't want their eyes to wander and we definitely don't want them to try another brand.

INITIAL LUST

Great business, like great relationships, is all about focusing energy, passion and thoughts into creating moments of total bliss and absolute pleasure. Iconic brands understand this and, like great lovers, have customers wanting to discover more, driving them crazy and holding them in a spell.

Long may the romancing continue...

> *"Go confidently in the direction of your dreams. Live the life you imagined"*
> Brian Tracey

About the Author

About the Author

Angi's retail pedigree is as diverse as it is distinguished – primarily with global household brands such as the Body Shop International, IKEA, Gap and M&S and finally with ESPA at Harvey Nichols & Liberty in London.

She has worked as a consultant with anything from cars, motorbikes, spectacles, skincare and wine merchants through to national charity organisations.

Within her retail career Angi gained knowledge and experience through successful senior management positions in all aspects that this multi-disciplined profession demands – operations, marketing, shop floor, manufacturing and finally retail merchandising.

Developing and refining her understanding from some of the best retailers, Angi quickly established herself as a natural retailer who loved nothing better than the thrill of seeing customers buy. She also recognised her innate capacity to lead and inspire individuals to achieve team and personal goals.

These are Angi's natural passions – retail and leadership – something she puts down to being 'proud to serve'. She discovered during her 20-year retail career that this requires dedication, courage, humility and commitment – some qualities she had in abundance, others she needed to discover through early mistakes.

With an instinctive feel for what works, what looks right and what will surprise and delight the customer, she is rapidly becoming recognised as one of the most innovative retail specialists. Her approach is contemporary, highly relevant and totally fresh, and her overriding priority is to maintain a laser-like focus on the commercial gains open to the retailer.

Based in the historic jewellery quarter in Birmingham, she works with businesses across the UK and internationally.

......
What People Say About Angi Egan

"Angi is a real joy to work with. She gets to the heart of customer feelings and how to practically reinforce their relationship with your services and brand. She did a great job visually revamping our reception and front office area, creating just the right atmosphere for our services for older people."
Michael Vincent, Chief Executive, Age Concern Coventry

"Angi makes you think. Makes you change. Makes you money."
Andy Clark, Founder and CEO of Speakers Academy

"Angi has an uncanny knack of finding all those winning ways and making them into compelling, easy-to-follow success strategies. She makes you wonder why they never seemed so obvious before she worked her magic!"
Gilbert Vasey, SpecSavers, Crystal Peaks, Sheffield

"Angi Egan has found an ingenious way of re-inventing an important 'business basic'. I have no hesitation in recommending her. She will exceed your expectations and you will probably feel motivated to give her a red rose and a box of chocolates!"
Phil Jesson, Director of Speaker Development,
The Academy for Chief Executives

"If there is one business book you should read this year it's this one! In these times, you need her informed insights into customer seduction more than ever."
Roger Harrop, President of the Professional Speakers Association

• • •